The David Carr Glover Christian Organ Library

The Church Musician

by
David Carr Glover
and
Phyllis Gunther

Alfred

FOREWORD

This *CHURCH MUSICIAN ORGAN REPERTOIRE* book is presented to supplement and reinforce the music fundamentals that the student is learning at this level of advancement. It is designed to be used with the *GRADED ORGAN COURSE, Learning to Play Church Organ Music — Level One.* However it may be used with any organ course or library.

Each book in this series presents standard hymns, some music of the masters, and original solos, which have been carefully selected and edited for gradual progress.

For additional materials to supplement *THE DAVID CARR GLOVER CHRISTIAN ORGAN LIBRARY, CONTEMPORARY ORGAN COURSE* is recommended.

REGISTRATIONS

A list of suggested registrations will be found on page 32 of this book, however, others could be used. In time the student should be required to create new ones.

MATERIALS CORRELATED WITH

CONTENTS

FDL 843

Chords and Pedal
C Major

The Dash Mark —

The dash mark in fingering, indicates the note it represents is tied.

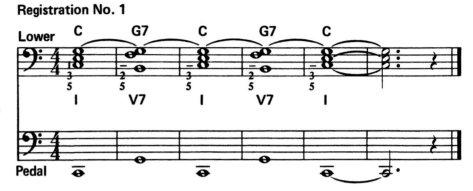

Thank You Song

GUNTHER

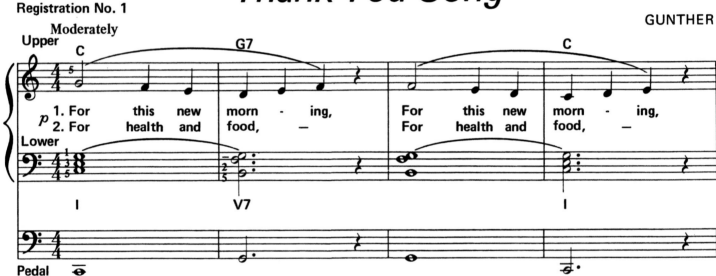

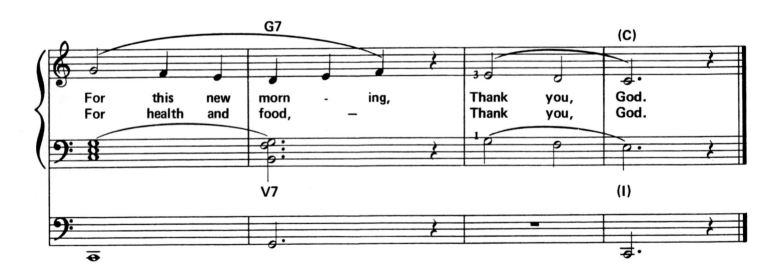

3. For love and friends,
   For love and friends,
   For love and friends,
   Thank you, God.

4. For all Your goodness,
   For all Your goodness,
   For all Your goodness,
   Thank you, God.

Two-Note Slurs

Sunday Morning

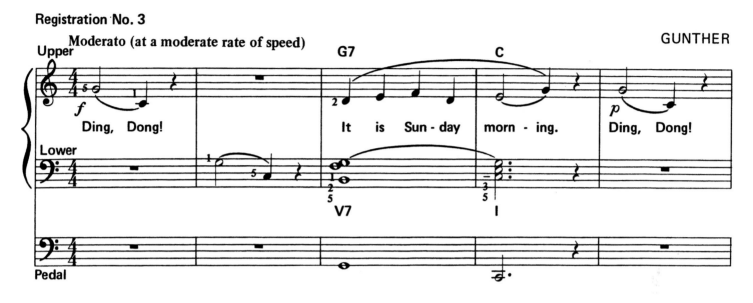

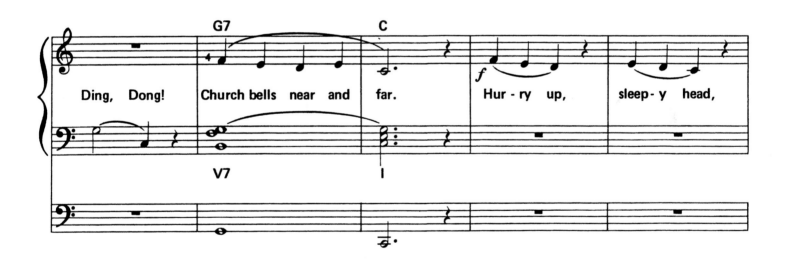

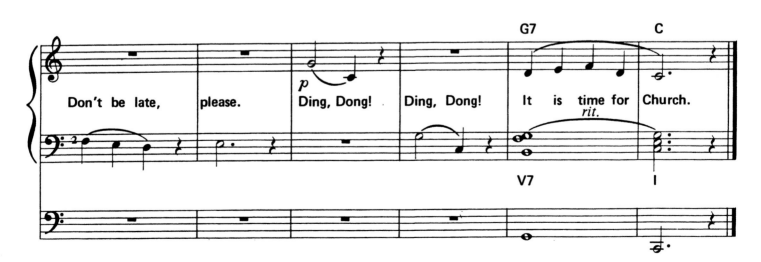

Interlude

During many church services, short interludes of music are used. Often an Interlude is played while worshipers proceed to their seats.

Interlude

GUNTHER

Morning Hymn

J. KEBLE, 1792–1866

LUDWIG van BEETHOVEN, 1770–1827

Note that both hands are on Treble staff.
Registration No. 4

Moderately

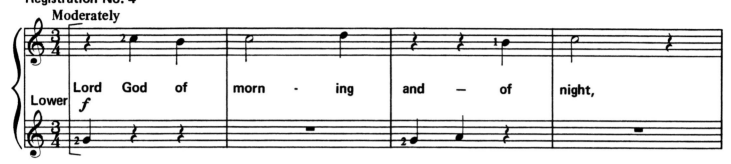

Lower Lord God of morn - ing and — of night,

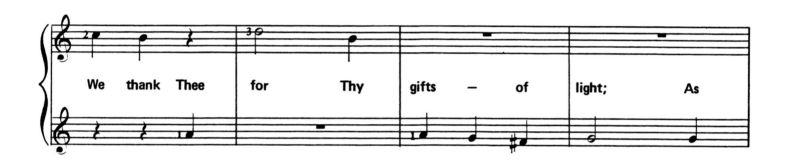

We thank Thee for Thy gifts — of light; As

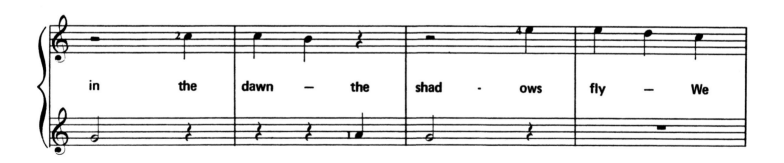

in the dawn — the shad - ows fly — We

seem to find — Thee now — more nigh.

FDL 843

Chords and Pedal
F Major

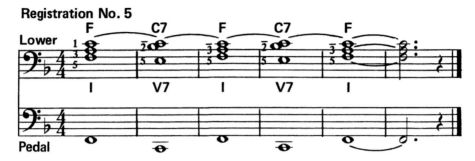

The word AMEN is used to close most hymns. Should the hymn have more than one stanza, usually the AMEN is used after the last stanza only. The use of the word AMEN which means "So be it" is an expression of reverent approval.

Oh, How I Love Jesus

ANONYMOUS

Breathe On Me, Breath of God

EDWIN HATCH, 1835–1889   ROBERT JACKSON, 1842–1914

Breathe On Me, Breath of God
Second Part

Stems Up: r.h.
Stems Down: l.h.

FDL 843

Can A Little Child Like Me?

MARY M. DODGE, 1831–1905

W. K. BASSWOOD, 1839–1902

Registration No. 4

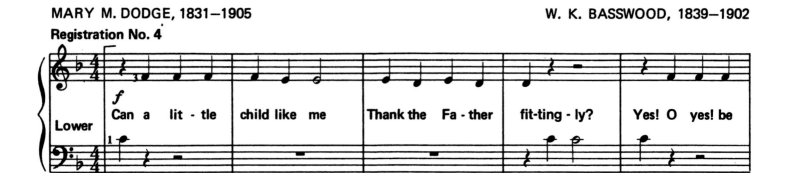

Lower — Can a lit - tle | child like me | Thank the Fa - ther | fit-ting - ly? | Yes! O yes! be

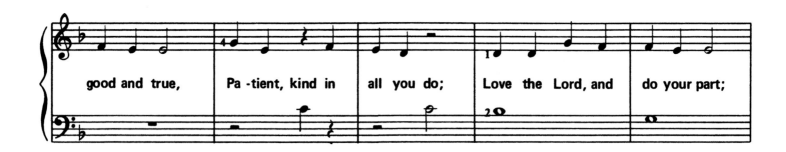

good and true, | Pa -tient, kind in | all you do; | Love the Lord, and | do your part;

Refrain:

Learn to say with | all your heart, | Fa - ther, we | thank Thee! | Fa - ther, we | thank Thee!

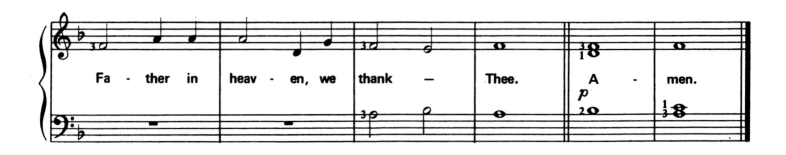

Fa - ther in | heav - en, we | thank — | Thee. | A - | men.

Pedal Solo

Registration No. 10

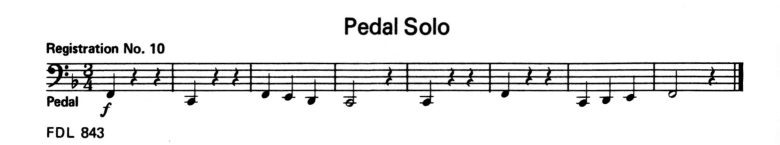

Pedal

FDL 843

All Praise to Thee

This hymn begins on the fourth beat of the measure. The missing three beats will be found in the last measure.

THOMAS KEN, 1637—1711

THOMAS TALLIS, 1505—1585

Hear Our Prayer

TRADITIONAL

Attributed to FREDERIC CHOPIN, 1810—1849

Staccato

A dot above ♪ or below ♪ a note means to play detached — not legato. This is called STACCATO.

mf —Mezzo Forte — Moderately Loud.   *mp* —Mezzo Piano — Moderately Soft.

Prelude
A Prelude is a composition usually played before the worship service. It may be repeated all or in part depending on the time remaining prior to the service. More than one Prelude may be used.

Prelude

Registration No. 6

Moderato

Adapted from CARL CZERNY, 1791—1857

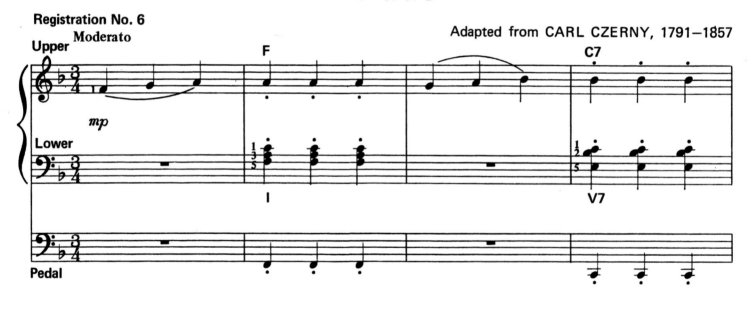

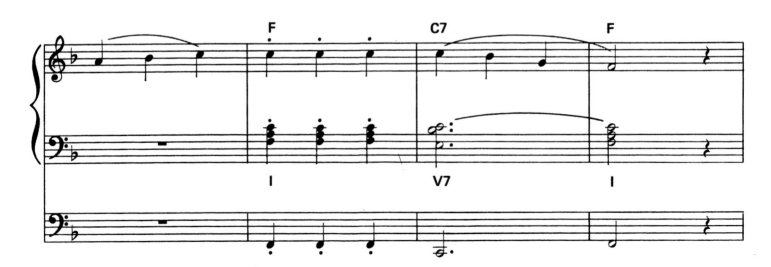

FDL 843

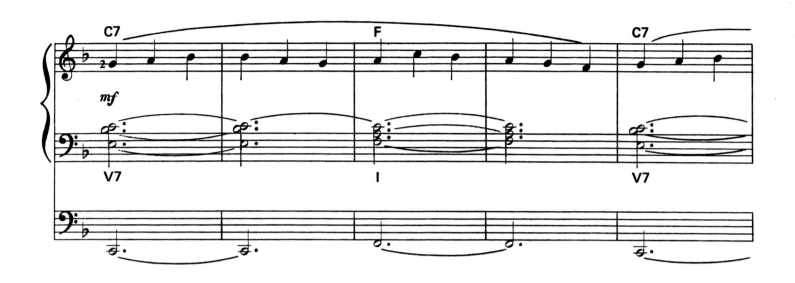

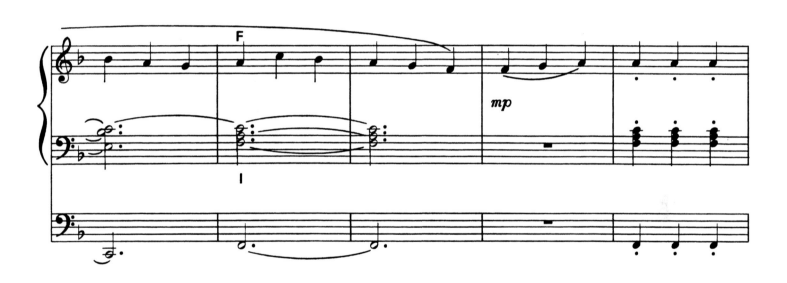

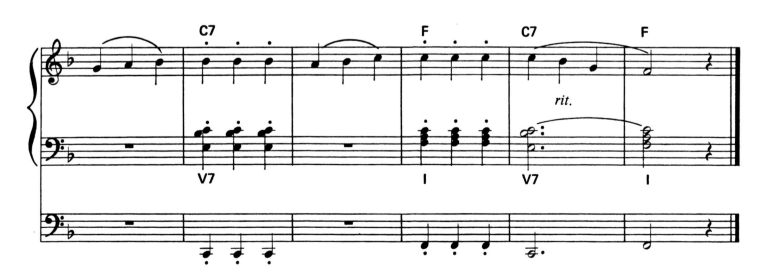

Chords and Pedal

G Major

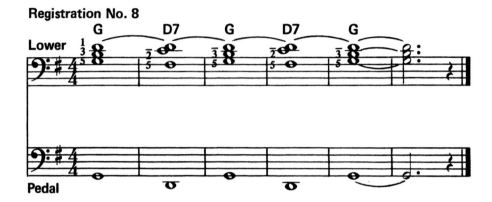

Holy God, We Praise Thy Name

Translated by C. WALWORTH, 1820—1903

CATHOLIC SONGBOOK, VIENNA 1774

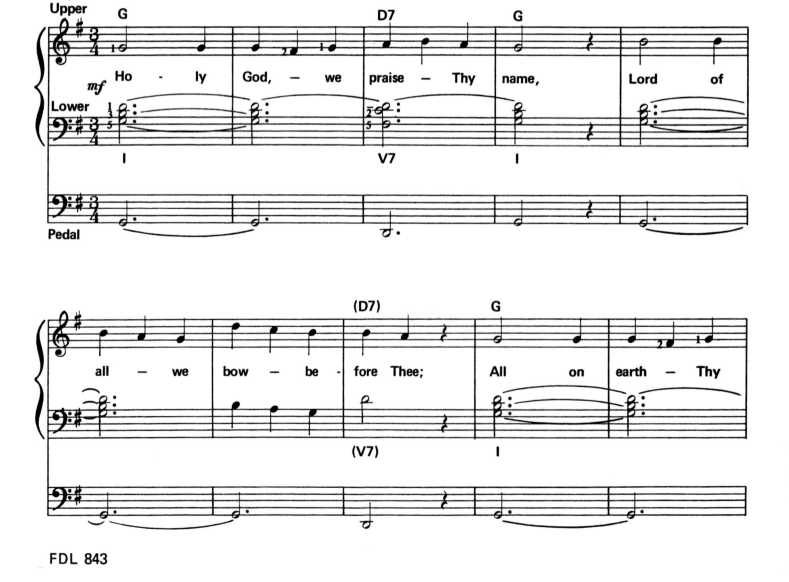

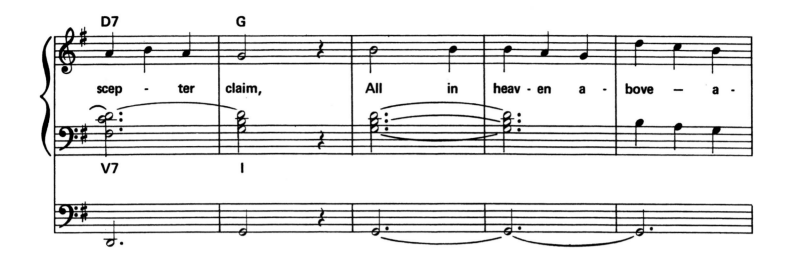

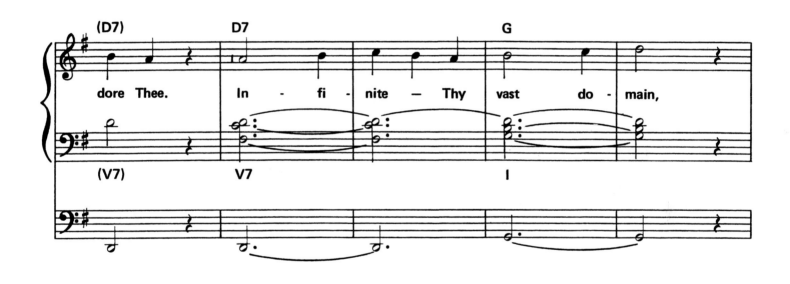

FDL 843

Oh, Worship the King

This hymn begins on the third beat of the measure. The missing first two beats will be found in the last measure.

SIR ROBERT GRANT, 1779—1838   GEORGE FREDERIC HANDEL, 1685—1759

Registration No. 4

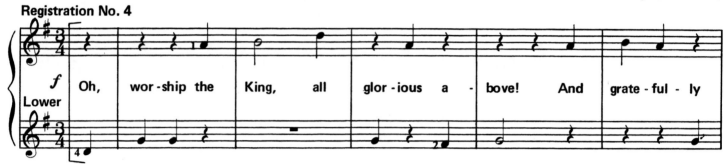

Oh, wor-ship the King, all glor-ious a-bove! And grate-ful-ly

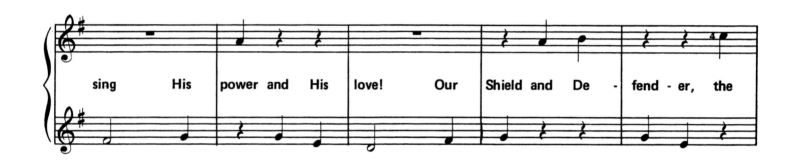

sing His power and His love! Our Shield and De-fend-er, the

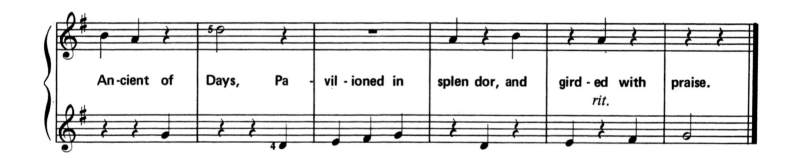

An-cient of Days, Pa-vil-ioned in splen dor, and gird-ed with praise.
rit.

Pedal Solo

Registration No. 10

Pedal *mf*

FDL 843

Transposition

Playing music in a different key from which it is written is called TRANSPOSING. See pages 17, 45 and 46 of the *GRADED ORGAN COURSE, Learning to Play Church Organ Music — Level One* for further information on Transposing.

Father, We Thank Thee

GUNTHER

Transpose "Father, We Thank Thee" into the major keys of C and F.

All Praise to God

GUNTHER

Transpose "All Praise to God" into the major keys of F and G.

FDL 843

Help Us, Lord

GUNTHER

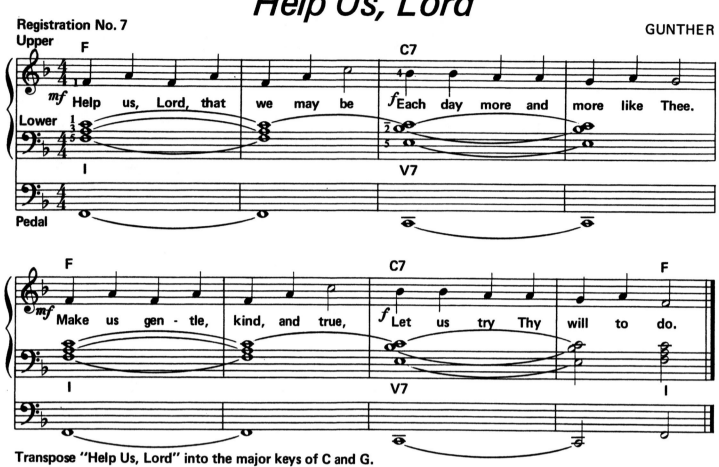

Registration No. 7
Upper
Lower
Pedal

mf Help us, Lord, that we may be *f* Each day more and more like Thee.

mf Make us gen-tle, kind, and true, *f* Let us try Thy will to do.

Transpose "Help Us, Lord" into the major keys of C and G.

Smiles of Our Father

L. C. LOCKLEY
Registration No. 8
Upper

W. J. KRAFT

Lower
Pedal

mf Smiles of our Fa - ther are sun - shine and rain;

mp Let us re - pay Him and smile back a - gain.

Transpose "Smiles of Our Father" into the major keys of C and F.
FDL 843

Eighth Note and Eighth Rest

♪ This is an EIGHTH NOTE. It receives ½ of a Beat when the quarter note receives one beat. Two or more Eighth Notes are written like this —

Two EIGHTH NOTES = one Quarter Note (♩) and receive 1 Beat.

♪ This is an EIGHTH REST. It has the same time value as one Eighth Note.

When He Cometh
(Precious Jewels)

WM. O. CUSHING, 1823–1902

GEORGE F. ROOT, 1820–1895

Registration No. 4

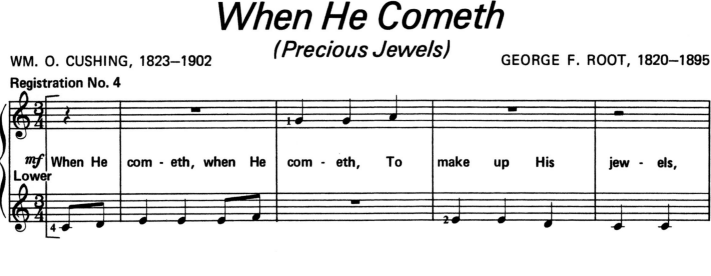

mf When He com - eth, when He com - eth, To make up His jew - els, Lower

All His jew - els, prec - ious jew - els, His loved and His own:

Refrain:

f Like the stars of the morn - ing, His — bright crown a - dorn - ing,

They shall shine in their beau - ty, Bright gems for His crown.

FDL 843

Natural

This is a NATURAL ♮ . It cancels a Sharp (♯) or a Flat (♭).

ff FORTISSIMO – Very Loud

pp PIANISSIMO – Very Soft

Let the Whole Creation Cry

STOPFORD A. BROOKE, 1832–1916

ROBERT WILLIAMS, 1781–1821

Registration No. 4

FDL 843

Accompanying

As an accompanist, in addition to being able to transpose music to keys other than written, the church musician should develop other skills which will make his performance more meaningful and interesting. When accompanying a congregation, play louder than when accompanying a soloist or a small group of people. Listen carefully as you accompany so that you may lend support to the singers rather than play so loudly that they cannot be heard. Also in accompanying a congregation, the accompanist must lead so that the tempo will not be too slow. However, when accompanying a soloist, the accompanist must follow rather than lead.

Happy the Home When God Is There

HENRY WARE JR., 1794–1843

JOHN B. DYKES, 1823–1876

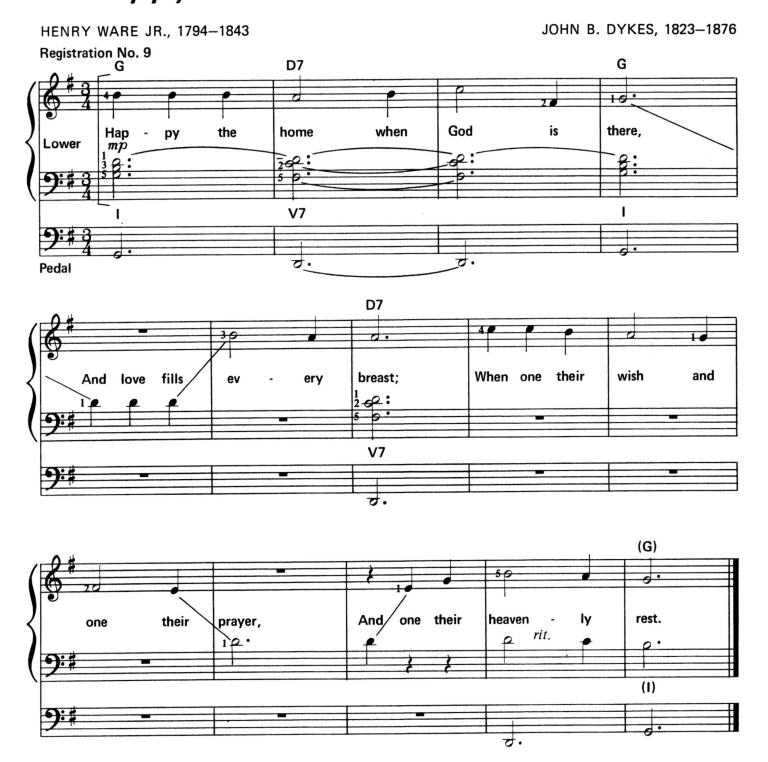

FDL 843

Cresc.	Dim.
(CRESCENDO)	(DIMINUENDO)
gradually play louder	gradually play softer

Offertory

An Offertory is a composition played while the offering is being collected. It may be repeated, all or in part depending on how much time is needed. It is usually played at a moderate speed and not too loud.

Offertory

GLOVER

Registration No. 2 (Omit Upper)

Moderately

Fermata

𝄐 **Hold longer than the time value of the note.**

Almighty Father, Hear Our Prayer

FELIX MENDELSSOHN, 1809–1847

Registration No. 1 (Omit Lower and Pedal)

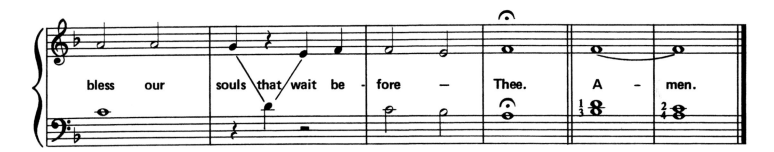

I'll Live for Him

R. E. HUDSON, 1843–1901

C. R. DUNBAR, 19th Century

Registration No. 9

FDL 843

Introduction

Usually the accompanist plays an introduction before the congregation sings. A form of introduction is to play through the entire hymn once. This is an excellent way for the congregation to become familiar with a new hymn before singing. It also allows time to find the music in the hymnal.

The following hymn is the oldest Christian hymn whose author is known. Clement of Alexandria wrote the words sometime between A. D. 202 and 220. It was written in the Greek language and was translated into English by Harry Dexter in 1846.

Shepherd of Tender Youth

CLEMENT OF ALEXANDRIA, 150—220 A.D.
Translated by HENRY M. DEXTER, 1821—1890

EDWARD BUNNETT, 1834—1923

Registration No. 8
Upper

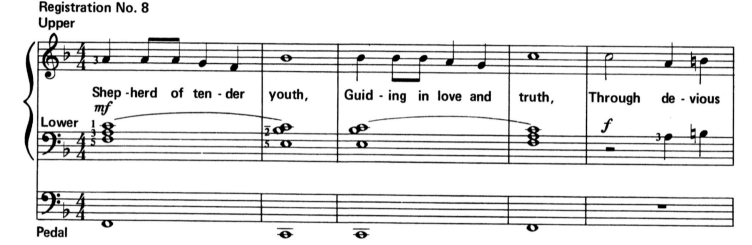

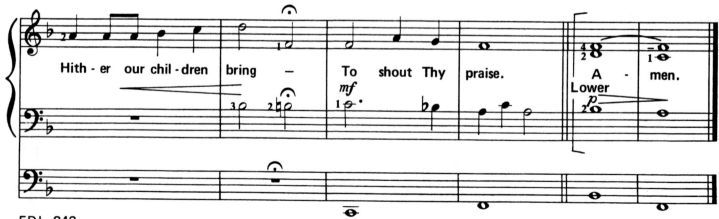

FDL 843

D. C. al Fine

D. C. (Da Capo) al Fine means return to the beginning and play to "Fine" (pronounced fee - nay).

Praise the Lord, His Glories Show

PSALM 148
HENRY F. LYTE, 1793–1847

JOSEPH D. JONES, 1827–1870

Pedal Solo

FDL 843

Accent Mark

> **>**   **Play Loudly**

Postlude

A Postlude is a composition played as the congregation leaves the church at the close of the worship service. If all the people have not left the church at the end of the Postlude, continue to play by repeating all or part of the piece.

Sometimes a suitable hymn tune may be played as a Postlude.

Lead On, O King Eternal

ERNEST W. SHURTLEFF, 1862–1917   HENRY SMART, 1813–1879

Registration No. 5 (Omit Lower)

THANKSGIVING

With Thankful Hearts, O Lord We Come

J. S. MOHLER, 19th Century

J. H. SHOWALTER, 1864–1947

Registration No. 6
Upper

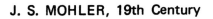

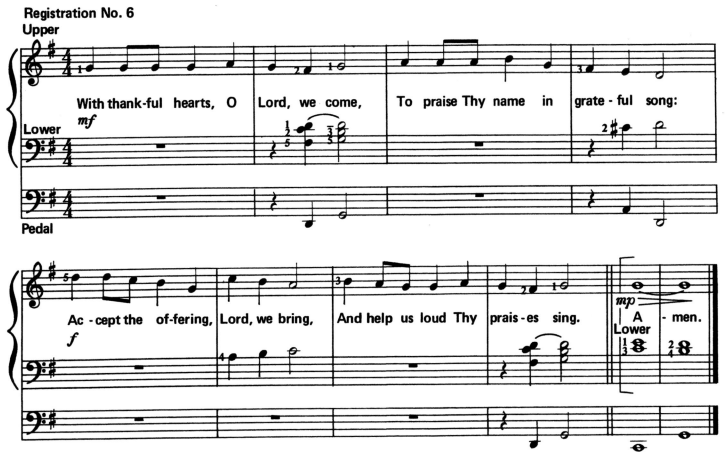

With thank-ful hearts, O Lord, we come, To praise Thy name in grate-ful song:

Ac-cept the of-fering, Lord, we bring, And help us loud Thy prais-es sing. A-men.

CHRISTMAS

Gospel Bells
(Bass Second Part)

Stems Up: r.h.
Stems Down: l.h.

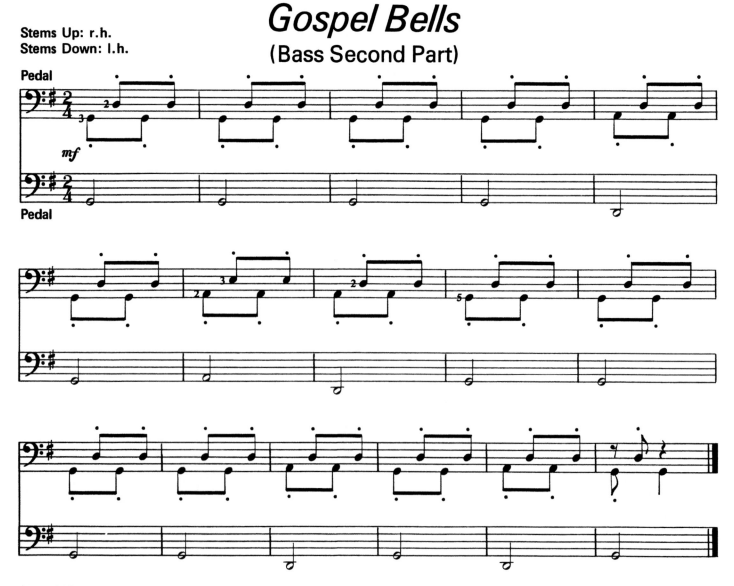

Gospel Bells
(To the Tune of Jingle Bells)

Treble First Part (Solo)

W. WILSON

J. S. PIERPONT

Registration No. 8

Gos - pel bells, Gos - pel bells, Ring them all the way, Ring them while you're

at your work and while you're at your play; Oh, Gos - pel bells, Gos - pel bells,

Ring them all the day, Ring the news that Je - sus came to take your sins a - way.

Gospel Bells
Second Part

Stems Up: r.h.
Stems Down: l.h.

For Introduction, play first four measures, then begin over again with other parts.

Gospel Bells can be played as a solo (omit Bass Player and Treble Second Player Parts); as a duet (use only one of the other two parts given); and as a trio (use all parts given). When played as a duet or trio, First Player (solo) waits for a four-measure introduction.

FDL 843

New Year

A. F. BROWN

E. KOHLER

Registration No. 5

Let the horns and whis-tles blow, so that all the world may know one more hap-py year has come, oh thank you Lord.

New Year

Second Part

Stems Up: r.h.
Stems Down: l.h.

Both hands 8va throughout.

EASTER

The Strife Is O'er

Translated from Latin by F. POTT, 1832–1909   *PALESTRINA, 1525–1594

Lyrics:
Alleluia! Alleluia! Alleluia!
The strife is o'er, the battle done; The victory of life is won; The song of triumph has begun. Alleluia! Amen.

*Information on Palestrina (Giovanni Pierluigi, called da Palestrina) will be found on page 43 of the *GRADED ORGAN COURSE, Learning to Play Church Organ Music — Level Five.*

FDL 843

Registrations

ELECTRONIC ORGANS	DRAWBAR ORGANS

1. Upper: Flutes 8', 4'
    Lower: String 8'
    Pedal: 16', 8'

    Ⓤ 00 7600 000
    Ⓛ 5443 2110
    Pedal 4

2. Upper: String 8', Flutes 8', 4'
    Lower: Diapason 8'
    Pedal: 16', 8'
    Vibrato on

    Ⓤ 00 7765 432
    Ⓛ 5641 1000
    Pedal 3
    Vibrato on

3. Upper: Flutes 16', 4'
    Lower: Flute 8'
    Pedal: 8', Soft
    Sustain on

    Ⓤ 00 5200 000
    Ⓛ 5432 1000
    Pedal 3
    Percussion on

4. Lower: Strings 8', 4', Horn 8'

    Ⓛ 8744 5550

5. Upper: Clarinet 8', String 8'
    Lower: Fr. Horn 8'
    Pedal: 16', 8'

    Ⓤ 00 7487 531
    Ⓛ 7665 0000
    Pedal 4

6. Upper: String 8'
    Lower: Flute 8'
    Pedal: 8'

    Ⓤ 00 7765 432
    Ⓛ 5432 2000
    Pedal 3

7. Upper: Trumpet 8'
    Lower: String 8'
    Pedal: 16', 8'

    Ⓤ 00 6688 888
    Ⓛ 4554 3210
    Pedal 4

8. Upper: String 8', Flutes 8', 4'
    Lower: 8' and 4' to balance
    Pedal: 16', 8'

    Ⓤ 00 7634 55
    Ⓛ 6654 4440
    Pedal 4

9. Lower: Diapason 8'
    Pedal: 16', 8'

    Ⓛ 6543 1000
    Pedal 4

10. Pedal Solo 16', 8'

    Pedal 4

TEACHER: Some adjustments will be necessary for each organ.